Car Cruiser supplemented their rakish beetle-backed streamlined caravans with more conventional models in the early 1930s. This is a 1934 Model 4, a 15 foot (4.6 metre) four-berth. It was built of 'steam-exploded, hard-pressed fibre' (hardboard, that is), and double-skinned walls were available at extra cost.

TOURING CARAVANS

Jon Pressnell

Shire Publications Ltd

CONTENTS

Printed in China through Worldprint Ltd.

British Library Cataloguing in Publication Data: Pressnall, Jon. Touring Caravans. 1. Caravans. I.
Title. 629. 226. ISBN-10 0 7478 0119 3. ISBN-13 978 0 74780 119 1.

Editorial Consultant: Michael E. Ware, Curator of the National Motor Museum, Beaulieu, Hampshire.

Cover: The Dragonfly, from a 1930s caravanning catalogue (courtesy of the author).

ACKNOWLEDGEMENTS
The majority of the photographs used come from the archives of *Caravan Magazine*; grateful thanks
to the editor, Barry Williams, for his kindness in making available this source. Thanks also to Jackie
Buist, editor of *Practical Caravan*, for her help with photographs, and to Edward Marriott at the
Caravan Club, Kim Hearn at Quadrant Picture Library, Joanne Battley at Omega, and Dave King at C. I.
Caravans. The photographs on pages 5, 8 (top and centre) and 10 are acknowledged to Quadrant/Autocar.

*'Gentlemen gypsies': a roadside halt for some members of the Caravan Club and their horse-drawn
gypsy caravan, some time before the First World War. Note the overhanging eaves and the (just
visible) lantern roof, characteristics carried through to early touring caravans.*

Frederick Alcock's streamlined caravan of 1914. Its shape was notably advanced and, in basic outline, could almost have come from the 1950s. The car is a 1913 38 horsepower Lanchester landaulet.

PRE-HISTORY: UP TO 1918

Contrary to popular wisdom, the caravan was *not* invented by gypsies: until the second half of the nineteenth century they used tents. The word 'caravan' as applied to wheeled vehicles had by the nineteenth century come to signify one of three things – a stage-wagon (rather lower down the scale than a stage-coach), a third-class train carriage, or a guard's van on a train.

The caravan as we know it seems to have emerged in around 1820-5, as a vehicle for travelling showmen. This usage spread, and by 1860 or so gypsies were indeed using horse-drawn caravans.

Two decades later the leisured classes discovered the caravan and began to affect the role of 'gentlemen gypsies'. The best known of these would-be Romanies was William Gordon-Stables, a naval surgeon and prolific writer of boys' and other books. He commissioned the building of what is today regarded as the first specifically recreational caravan, *The Wanderer*. In 1886 he set off in this 2 ton luxury 'land yacht', with a tricycle-mounted valet as advance guard, to tour Britain. He wrote a book about his experiences, *The Cruise of the Land Yacht Wanderer*, which did much to publicise caravanning.

In 1907 the Caravan Club was founded, to cater for the growing breed of 'gentlemen gypsies'. Despite the advance of motoring in the years before the First World War, the club remained emphatically devoted to the horse-drawn caravan – an attitude that was to bring about its near-terminal decline by the 1930s, before it reversed its policy just in time.

Before the First World War a trailer caravan was a horse-drawn caravan. Motor caravanning in its infancy meant a motor van – in other words a caravan body mounted on a car or commercial chassis. The first such vehicle, called a *maison automobile*, was shown in Paris in 1904, and in 1909 the first motor van to be displayed in Britain was exhibited at the Motor Show; others followed.

The first trailer caravan for motor cars is thought to have been made by Frederick Alcock, who built a 'streamlined' vehicle in 1914 for towing behind his 1913 Lanchester. It was notably advanced for the period but it was to remain unique until after the First World War.

3

Right: *The original Eccles trailer caravan of 1919. It was intended to be used not just for holidays, but also as a mobile doctor's or dentist's surgery in remote areas. The colour scheme was dark green with a stone-coloured roof — not very practical, as these dark colours absorbed heat rather than reflected it.*

Left: *Within a couple of years the basic Eccles had evolved into this less austere form, with overhanging eaves. Joined in 1923 by the lantern-roofed 'de luxe' model, it continued throughout the decade. Panelling was in canvas-covered plywood, painted, or at extra cost in steel-armoured ply; double walling was optional, and interior woodwork on all but the smallest model could be French-polished to either a light or a mahogany finish.*

Right: *An early Piggott caravan from around 1922. The sides are made of fabric, and the whole caravan dismantles. Piggott's largest model, 17 feet (5.18 metres) long, featured a pull-out platform at the rear, forming a verandah when used in conjunction with a canvas awning.*

Possibly the first post-First World War caravan. Captain St Barbe Baker sets off for a tour of Europe, in August 1920, in the caravan he built the previous year entirely from aeroplane parts. The tow-car is a modified Model T Ford.

EARLY YEARS: 1918-30

The trailer caravan to emerge after the First World War was inspired from four main sources: the wartime utility trailer, the horse-drawn caravan, the aeroplane, and finally the motor caravan. These sources came together mainly because Britain after the Armistice had a large pool of practically minded ex-servicemen with an experience of motor vehicles and an understanding of the potential of the Army surplus materials then readily available.

Typical of those pioneer caravans was that built by Captain St Barbe Baker of the Royal Flying Corps. Constructed entirely of aeroplane parts, it appeared in June 1919 and is regarded as the first post-First World War trailer caravan. Other caravans were produced in the same year by Eccles, Guildford, Grosvenor and others, followed in 1920 by Piggott.

The original Eccles, announced in December 1919, was a crude box on wheels made of soldered-together sheets of steel, with polished oak or mahogany inner walls and two 6 foot 6 inch (1.98 metre) beds, a tip-up basin and a toilet locker. It followed on from a motor van built in 1913 and was intended as a diversification from the main Eccles business of road haulage.

The respected tent-makers Piggott were another early manufacturer to receive extensive publicity. Their ingenious caravans ranged in length from 9 feet (2.74 metres) to 17 feet (5.18 metres) and were based in their original form on a light wood framework built around the two box-girders forming the seats and bed-boxes; over this framework canvas sides were laced, and the whole structure was held together by bolts and wing-nuts, to allow easy dismantling.

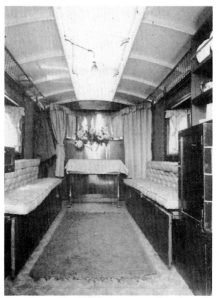

As others began making caravans, such as Fleming-Williams, with his novel streamlined Car Cruiser, the caravanning movement began to gather a following. Indeed, it was referred to as a 'vogue', perhaps a little over-optimistically, as early as 1920. Leading the way, if coverage in the magazines is any guide, appear to have been Eccles and Piggott, but by 1921 another soon to be respected firm had arrived on the scene – Bertram Hutchings, a builder of horse-drawn caravans since 1912.

In 1923 came an important landmark in the development of the caravan: Eccles introduced a new and less austere model, with a lantern roof (a roof with a raised centre section to give extra headroom, in the style of horse-drawn caravans) and berths for four, in two double beds. As their range expanded, Eccles became the industry leader, and in 1927 they established the first factory in Britain expressly built for caravan manufacture.

Interior of a 1924 Piggott, showing the simplicity of the fittings and the railway-carriage ambience.

By this time the Austin Seven was a regular sight on British roads, and two years

Bertram Hutchings was one of the first makers of caravans and was to play a dominant role in their history. This is probably his first touring caravan and dates from 1921. It is clearly derived from earlier horse-drawn models.

An Eccles 'de Luxe', with lantern roof. Drawing on the horse-drawn caravan for its body design, it promoted a style which almost became an industry norm in the 1920s. It was built of plywood over a wooden frame and in 9 foot (2.74 metre) form cost £218 in 1926, when a basic two-seater Morris Cowley was costing £162 10s.

later came Morris's riposte, the Minor. The new small cars led to smaller and thus cheaper caravans suitable for being towed behind such vehicles.

Another response to these smaller cars, and to the need to dispel hesitant motorists' fears about caravans and their bulk, was the introduction of collapsible and folding caravans. These became, for a while, an important part of the caravanning scene, and by the end of the decade makers such as Eccles were offering most of their models in both rigid and collapsible form. One of the leading producers, Rice, claimed that their popular fabric-sided folding caravan could be erected in one minute.

Caravanning in Britain was, however, still in its infancy – especially when compared to the United States, where the more rapid spread of the motor car had inevitably boosted caravanning.

There was a strong enthusiasm, but a lack of a single vision for the caravan. On the one hand there were austere lightweight trailer tents, on the other massive and often unstable 'mobile cottages', *folies de grandeur* which seemed to be designed with no thought of whether or not any car could safely tow them. The bigger and more ambitious of these caravans used twin axles and were sometimes attached inboard, in the fashion of an articulated lorry, to the back of a car specifically modified for the purpose. Such vans were built to special order, often for foreign clients, and were a graphic illustration of the importance of one-off caravans to the industry – half the output of Eccles by the end of the 1920s was to special order.

The sense of whimsy behind the mobile cottages with their pitched roofs and bay windows was only part of the romanticism attached to caravanning in the 1920s. En-

7

Left: *One of the earliest of the collapsible caravans, the Shadow was first seen in 1928. To raise the upper half, a winding mechanism was used. Accommodation was for four, two settees converting into four bunk beds. Note the front bay window – a typical bit of 1920s whimsy.*

Below: *This one-off Eccles was built for an American customer. The caravan was 18 feet (5.49 metres) long and was mounted on a turntable built on to the rear of the tow-car, a coupé constructed on a GMC light commercial chassis. Hot and cold water came from an 85 gallon (386.4 litre) tank, and there was also a shower and a refrigerator, electric lighting and a wireless.*

Below: *One of the more flamboyant streamlined caravans in the 1920s was the Car Cruiser. Despite the aerodynamic advantages claimed for its shape, in the following decade the makers moved away from streamlining. In the early years construction was of waterproofed canvas over a wooden framework. The photograph shows a c.1935 model, but it is basically the same as those current at the end of the 1920s.*

A rather unstable-looking 'mobile cottage' from the mid 1920s. Such conceits were very much a part of the caravanning scene at the time.

thusiastic caravanners were forever talking of being 'motor gypsies' or of savouring the 'gypsy joys' of caravanning. But the 'health, happiness, and novel experiences to be acquired under the blue vault of heaven', to quote one caravanning romanticist, were generally not sufficiently alluring to tempt early motorists into buying their own caravan – even if they could afford to do so. The existence of hire fleets of caravans was thus of crucial importance in the development of caravanning, and as late as 1932 at least fourteen makers were running their own hire fleets.

A further sign of the infancy of the cara-

vanning movement was the absence of formal caravan sites, in which Britain also lagged behind the United States, where by the early 1920s towns were providing municipal sites. In Britain caravanners either camped 'wild', wherever there was a convenient spot for their caravan, or else asked permission of a farmer or landowner to set up in one of his fields. In a five-week tour of Scotland in 1925 one couple did not stay in a single formal site.

By 1929 there was, however, a feeling of consolidation. The touring caravan seemed to have arrived as an accepted part of the motoring scene, as evidenced by *The Autocar*

The proportions were not quite right on the 1930 Eccelite, but the caravan was to lead Eccles in a new direction for the 1930s, towards a caravan shape which was to remain largely unchanged for several decades.

carrying out for the first time a market survey of the caravan industry.

That caravans were moving into a new era was demonstrated by the announcement by Bertram Hutchings of his revolutionary Winchester in 1930. Its shape, blending square-rigged practicality with limited streamlining, had considerable impact. It was followed by the Eccles Eccelite. Within a season the Eccelite had developed into a more modern shape. This led Eccles in 1931 to fuse its two strands of design – the traditional, with its roots in horse-drawn caravans, and the more streamlined modern, as shown in the lines of the Eccelite – into a fresh identity for the new decade.

The year 1930 was a turning point, an important and productive year, as the attention given to caravans in the following twelve months bears out. Despite the developing tension between cleaner and squarer lines on one hand and streamlining on the other, the industry was poised to enter an exciting decade, in which the trailer caravan was finally to become an established part of the motoring world.

The Winchester by Bertram Hutchings (on the right) featured modest streamlining and showed the way forward in caravan design. It was appreciably more elegant than the square-cut caravan also from Hutchings accompanying it in this 1930/1 photograph.

10

Bertram Hutchings, creator of the Winchester caravan, taking the hairpin during the driving tests at the 1933 RAC Caravan Rally at Cheltenham. The caravan is a development of the original Winchester shape and features a streamlined lantern roof.

THE 1930s

As the new decade opened, the traditional shape of caravan was being supplanted, as streamlined lantern roofs and the rounded 'aero' look became ever more popular. Sometimes streamlining was carried almost too far, with bizarre results in terms of both aesthetics and practicality, but in this the caravan industry was only reflecting the similar process taking place in car design at the same time.

A major impetus to the growth of caravanning in the 1930s came from the development of clubs and rallies, particularly in 1932 and 1933. In 1932 the first national caravan rally since the days of horse-drawn caravans took place at Minehead, Somerset, promoted by *The Autocar*. The magazine extensively publicised the event, which was attended by ninety caravans, over a quarter of which were entered by the trade.

As a showcase for the industry the rally achieved a great deal, and despite the slump almost all manufacturers reported a signi-ficant increase in sales, while the Royal Automobile Club (RAC) estimated that during 1932 it received over 1800 enquiries about caravanning and arranged over two thousand sites. This impressed the organisation sufficiently for it to take over the running of the 1933 rally, which took place at Cheltenham.

In 1932 also the Junior Car Club (JCC), a motor-sport club, set up its own caravan section, and the Camping Club enrolled three hundred new members, prompting it the next year to form a separate caravan section and hold its first all-caravan rally. The Caravan Club was reconstituted in 1935 and a year later absorbed the JCC's caravan section. By the end of the decade the two clubs were thriving and had been joined by various clubs catering for specific makes of caravan; after the Second World War, these one-make clubs were to become an important element in the social side of caravanning.

11

A Raven Argonette caravan with a Vale Special sports car – a real rarity. The Argonette was introduced in 1933, for tow-cars such as the Austin Seven and Morris Minor. A 9 foot (2.7 metre) two-berth, it weighed only $5^1/2$ cwt (279 kg). Its curved lines are typical of Ravens of the period.

A further major fillip to the popularity of the caravan was the increasing press attention given to caravanning, with *The Autocar* introducing a regular column on the subject in 1932, and with the launch of the world's first caravan magazine, *Caravan and Trailer*, a year later. The new journal was to wield a considerable influence, as it prompted the re-formation of the Caravan Club and served as the re-born club's official mouthpiece.

As the decade advanced, caravan design moved towards a new maturity, with streamlining excesses eventually curbed and, by 1939, a general consensus on the caravan's shape, which would now remain broadly unchanged through to the end of the 1950s.

Before that, however, there was a period of exuberant creativity, typified by such caravans as the curvaceous Carlight and the Art Deco influenced Airlite, with its starburst leaded windows and bold sweeping side mouldings. Others were striking less for their style than for their configuration. In

particular, there was a rash of caravans with extending sides.

The County caravan, on the other hand, was unusual in that one side hinged up in the manner of a canteen serving hatch; it also differed from the norm in being built out into a triangle at both ends, and having a tow-bar at each extremity, so it could be towed from either end.

The construction of caravans also evolved during this period. The first generation of touring caravans had generally been built around a substantial stress-bearing timber floor, rather than a chassis as such, and they were usually panelled in plywood covered with a waterproofed fabric, with a roof of ply covered with fabric bedded in white lead. Sometimes the main walls were made of plywood faced with steel or alloy, but this was not widespread. During the 1930s, however, pressed fibreboard gradually displaced plywood, and steel chassis, often of a proprietary make, were used in place of the stress-bearing timber floor-cum-frame.

Exterior protection came from up to ten

Right: *More conservative in style, and with a basic shape which would remain current until the 1950s, is this 1933 Eccles, a 10 foot (3 metre) two-berth. Cost in 1933 was £105, as against £85 for the Raven Argonette.*

Left: *The products of some manufacturers remained relatively upright and austere in style well into the 1930s. This is a 1935 Ensor with a folding kitchen. Note the bay window and the dated artillery wheels.*

Right: *A large Carlight displays the characteristically rounded lines of the make and the unusual way in which the lantern roof is carried through to the caravan tail. The photograph dates from 1937. Carlight still exists, and its caravans are regarded as the ultimate hand-built luxury tourers.*

13

The freakish and extravagant Rollalong Streamer dates from 1936 and features an odd square-cut add-on rear section with double doors. Equipment included a hot water shower, a sunken bath and two movable easy chairs convertible into beds. Cost was £325, half as much again as the price of the Ford V8 used as a tow-car.

coats of paint (although five was more normal), with a luxury caravan perhaps using a total of 1 cwt (50 kg) of paint, including the white lead used to bed down the roof canvas, a practice which generally continued, as alternatives such as leathercloth, either directly pinned to the roof or laid over padding, proved unsuccessful in service.

The body frame still tended to be of ash wood, for its strength and lightness, and on the more expensive caravans curved members were bought in from specialists who had steamed and bent them to shape; cheaper caravans used timber sawn from the solid, which doubtless explains why they tended to have less curvaceous contours. Frames used proper joints, sometimes plated; it was

particularly important that care was taken over the joints if the caravan were a single-skinned model. Double-skinning, with the caravan having an inner and an outer wall, did, however, become usual as the decade progressed, as it improved the insulation of the caravan against the elements.

The inner skin could be of ply, hardboard or insulation board and was painted, figured or perhaps even veneered. Underneath, though, the wood and the joinery might well be inferior to those used when the wood was visible.

To improve insulation, occasionally the cavity between the two skins was lined with foil or some form of insulating material such as latex, cork, glass-fibre wool or

The splendid Art Deco Car Cruiser is a 1938 16 foot (4.9 metre) model. Features included double walls with aluminium foil insulation, an 'emergency commode', a meat safe, full sets of cutlery and crockery, and kitchen equipment ranging from a set of saucepans to a milk can. Heating, lighting and cooking were by Calor gas.

14

kapok, while a bitumen and cork underlay was often found under the linoleum covering the floor. Some caravans even had 'treble insulated' walls, with air spaces either side of the insulating material.

There was little technical progress during the 1930s, beyond the introduction of the ball-hitch in place of the crude pin type of coupling. Despite a greater interest in towing stability, dampers were still rarely fitted, and beam axles remained normal, generally cranked to allow a lower floor and an improved centre of gravity.

The interior of a 1938 Eccles. Note the opening panes in the lantern roof, the floor-to-ceiling furniture, the rounded corners to some units, and the provision of both gas and electric lighting. Post-war vans would tend to be rather more austere.

Instead, the emphasis was on the provision of a high level of internal and external equipment. The fitting of a jockey wheel to aid manoeuvring and of hydraulic corner-steadies were valid improvements but elaborate gas heating and hot and cold water systems, wireless sets, full electrical installations and even baths set into the bed lockers were conceits that added to the weight and size of the caravan and, while satisfying an owner's pride at his club's rallies, did little to advance the cause of caravanning.

These facilities were mostly found on costly one-off caravans built to special order. More relevant were the smaller and more modestly priced family caravans, not least those 10 foot (3 metre) models introduced in response to the boom in 10 horsepower cars. Some of the cheaper caravans were crude in design and construction and made by small firms with poor chances of long-term survival, but such models did further open up the market.

A portent for the future was the introduction in 1939 of the Eccles National, a 14½ foot (4.4 metre) double-skinned four-berth caravan retailing at only £130. Batch-built and jig-assembled according to a streamlined production process, it heralded a new kind of cheap series-production family caravan and stood in marked contrast to caravans such as the Winchester, which were individually constructed by craftsmen, to high coachbuilding standards.

Coventry Steel was one of those manufacturers to buck convention, and this 1938 Silent Knight had steel panels covered with felt and then with an outer skin of leathercloth. For 1939 the leathercloth was replaced by aluminium. In the post-war years the firm was to continue with unusual forms of construction.

15

The Streamlite Rover of 1947 was built of Holoplast partitioning material intended for housing and used Spitfire fighter-aircraft landing wheels, with a Spitfire tail wheel as a jockey wheel – typical of the improvisations necessary because of post-war materials shortages.

THE SECOND WORLD WAR AND ITS AFTERMATH

The Second World War played an important part in the development of the caravan; much more crucial, however, were the aftermath of the war and the response of the caravan industry to the demanding conditions of post-war Britain.

After an initial failure to appreciate the value of caravans in wartime, the authorities soon began to make extensive use of them. As temporary accommodation for evacuees and mobile billets for soldiers, caravans were ideal, while they also lent themselves to conversion into ambulances and mobile canteens. And so a new type of caravan was introduced: short, upright boxes on wheels, such as the Raven 'Mobile Billet', equipped with nothing more than sets of bunks and a washbasin.

These wartime vans were made at a time of shortages and consequently new products and techniques had to be used because traditional materials were not available. 'Composition board' (chipboard) took the place of plywood, and sometimes constructors had to make do with softwood, which added to the bulk and weight of the caravan's panelling. Most chassis were of wood, with the unfortunate result, on some caravans, that a sagging timber chassis would pull away the inner panels from their joints, thereby letting in water. Furthermore, because demand was heavy, unscrupulous concerns sprang up, selling shoddily built, leak-prone caravans to unsuspecting homeless people desperate for a roof over their heads.

Beneficial changes, however, included the wartime development of new glues, facilitating jointing, and the growth in jig-assembly and the use of laminated bends rather than carved-from-the-whole timber members. In addition, because a caravan needed to be suitable for all-year-round living, serious attention was given to insulation and the single-skin caravan began to be phased out.

With the end of the war, the immediate need was for caravans as accommodation, to house both the bombed-out homeless and the communities of workers needed for reconstruction projects. As early as April 1945 *The Autocar* reported sixty or so caravans parked down a single stretch of a London bypass, and it was not long before shanty towns of caravans, often makeshift home-built models, were springing up. These ramshackle sites, lacking facilities and having dubious proprietors, did much to raise hostility to the caravan, and caravan sites became a contentious issue for many years.

The caravan, which before the war had been an adjunct to motor touring, now became primarily a permanent and non-mobile residence: in 1946 Eccles revealed that 72 per cent of their output was being supplied for residential use, and in 1950 industry sources estimated that 80 per cent of caravans built since the war were being used, or had been used, as permanent homes.

All this led to a blurring of the distinction between touring and residential caravans. The latter were often made to resemble tourers, and it was claimed, for instance, that a 22 foot (6.7 metre) residential van, with an unladen weight of 39 cwt (1980 kg), could double as a touring caravan. What motor car could safely tow such a trailer was not explained.

Meanwhile, despite the boom in demand, the industry was struggling. The needs of the building industry meant that ash (for caravan frames), plywood and hardboard (for exterior panelling) were all scarce – and indeed were rationed.

Allocation was on the basis of pre-war export performance, and before the war British caravans had not generally been exported; at one stage in 1947 it was decided that the caravan industry would have no allocations for the coming year. Eventually an allocation was agreed, tied to a requirement to export 20 per cent of production, but with supply problems continuing, the industry had to look to alternative materials and to government surplus.

Thus the 1947 Streamlite Rover, for instance, was built from Holoplast, a double-skinned plastic honeycomb material intended for partitioning in houses, and used

Burlingham, a quality make from the pre-war years, was offering this 'Sportsman' model in 1948. Unusual features include the downward slope of the roof and the roof-mounted boat supplied as standard.

Car Trailers continued to offer their characteristic sunflap on their post-war models, but now it was at the rear, and little more than a large lift-up window. This model is an early 1950s 14 foot (4.3 metre) four-berth Countess. Note the generous lantern roof.

landing wheels from Spitfire fighter planes, with Spitfire tail wheels serving as jockey wheels.

Above all, the industry turned to aluminium, which was not on allocation, and by the end of the 1940s most manufacturers were using it for exterior panelling, as well as for window framing in place of the previously used chromed brass.

Unfortunately, few understood how to assemble alloy sheet to avoid problems of expansion and contraction under temperature changes, or of sacrificial corrosion when alloy abutted steel; nor had many mastered the techniques of painting aluminium so that the paint adhered to the metal. In addition, unsupported alloy sheet all too often resulted in wavy panels.

It was a disaster, and as soon as hardboard, which was up to three times cheaper, became available, manufacturers returned to the material with which they were most familiar – perforce, for a while, during the Korean War, when there were aluminium shortages. Unfortunately post-war hardboard was often of inferior quality, resulting in fresh problems with cockling and warping.

Well into the 1950s the industry alternated between aluminium and hardboard, as on the one hand hardboard became of better quality and on the other manufacturers came to master aluminium, with its better durability; some offered hardboard panelling as standard, with aluminium available at extra cost. A common compromise was to use aluminium for the roof, where it had considerable advantages over the traditional fabric-over-hardboard construction, and perhaps for the end panels, and to retain hardboard, possibly of the ready-finished stove-enamelled variety, for the side panels.

Design creativity was not entirely absent in these straightened early post-war years, although more often than not it was restricted to the residential caravans which dominated the market.

One particular innovation tried by various makers was to construct the caravan from alloy panels riveted together. Noteworthy here are the Silver Knight, using interlocking vertical alloy strips, and the Overlander, which was in effect an alloy monocoque, with a floor made of alloy trays riveted one to another.

A Safari Minor from 1948 – a small two-berth with the unusual feature of two front-end doors. Safari caravans established their reputation with larger models of high quality and traditional style.

Paladin promoted their 8 foot 6 inch (2.6 metre) Pixy of 1952 as a 'super lightweight' – it weighed 8½ cwt (432 kg) and had hardboard panels.

Typical Coventry Steel extravagance: the 1950 Silver Knight. The body used interlocking vertical alloy strips, obviating the need for conventional framing.

Although they were residential caravans, the 1946 Shrager Carapartment and the 1953 Montrose Castle were important technologically. The former, later renamed the Berkeley Baronet, had walls made of a bonded sandwich of aluminium outer, Onazote cellular rubber centre and plywood inner, while the Montrose Castle had sandwich-construction sides made of glue-impregnated corrugated cardboard bonded between hardboard inner and outer walls – a light and strong method of construction which was a forerunner of the sandwich techniques to become dominant in the 1980s.

Ever keen to try something different, in 1952 Coventry Steel produced the Tickford Knight. Each side wall was made of a single sheet of resin-laminated marine-ply, with the entire shell bonded together with synthetic resin glues; it was claimed that not a single screw or nail was used in the body's construction.

Thomson was a respected Scottish firm which began making touring caravans in the 1920s. The V roof was long a characteristic of the make and was found to have aerodynamic advantages. Shown is a two-berth Carron, from 1953/4.

THE 1950s

As the 1950s progressed, the touring caravan returned to prominence, with the revival and expansion of leisure caravanning and the growing interest in continental touring.

One key result was the emergence of a new kind of manufacturer, concentrating on cheap touring caravans for a new clientele. Famous names from the 1930s such as Winchester and Car Cruiser became very minor participants in the boom years of the later 1950s, as aggressive new firms such as Bluebird and Alperson turned out cheap caravans by the thousand.

Bluebird had begun before the war, producing shoddy, low-cost caravans which were sold without any recognised brand name. Through bulk buying of materials, assembly-line production with extensive jigging, and 24 hour production in peak periods, the firm shook off much of its poor reputation and became the major producer of cheap caravans, both touring and static, by the end of the 1950s. It claimed in 1958 to be 'the largest caravan organisation in the world' and boasted of a weekly production of between two hundred and three hundred caravans – at a time when Car Cruiser were making a mere one hundred bespoke tourers per *year*.

It was Alperson, though, who were to have a more durable success, under the leadership of the dynamic Sam Alper. Realising that the market for his Streamlite Rover was limited, at a price of £575 in 1949 (£190 more than a Morris Minor), that year he devised a simple hardboard-panelled 11 foot (3.35 metre) box on wheels, which he dubbed the Sprite. Costings indicated a retail price of £235, but Alper decided to sell the Sprite at £199 and use this low price to create a market for the new caravan.

Despite initial resistance from the trade, the Sprite soon established itself, partly as a result of Alper's well publicised long-distance continental tours in his caravans – activities which convinced the sceptical of the durability of the product. Other Sprite models followed, and annual production leapt from under one thousand in 1952 up to 2500 in 1957, reaching over five thousand by 1960.

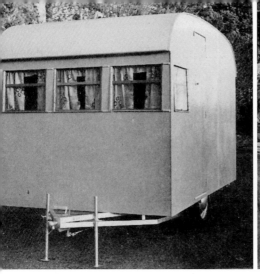

Left: *Bluebird began as makers of cut-price vans of dubious quality. This Bluebird Bantam from the late 1940s or early 1950s certainly shows signs of being a crude product.*

Right: *How caravans used to be built. Workmen at the Berkeley factory assemble the wooden side frames in their jigs. Greater automation and the introduction of sandwich construction put an end to such labour-intensive working practices.*

The shift in emphasis towards touring caravans led to a renewed interest in weight-saving, aided by the need to create caravans suitable for towing by the new generation of small cars such as the Standard Eight, Morris Minor and Austin A30.

Now with greater confidence in the material, manufacturers turned to thinner gauges of aluminium, ribbing it to give extra strength. Thinner hardboard was used for internal panels, too, and the chassis and the floor were treated more as a single unit, resulting in a less substantial chassis, as the floor was allowed to take more of the van's strength. One manufacturer, Pearman Briggs, even dispensed with the chassis on their Safari model, using a glued and screwed box-section structure incorporating bed-lockers to serve as floor and chassis combined.

Lighter-weight caravans and the growth in continental touring also gave an impetus to technical advance, aided by a similar process taking place in the motor industry at the same time. The major step forward in this area was the introduction of independ-

The Alperson Streamlite Sprite opened up new markets for the caravan. Cheap and cheerful, yet with independent suspension, it soon proved its robustness when taken on high-mileage continental publicity trips by its creator, Sam Alper.

Right: *Charles Panter's Berkeley concern was one of the leading innovators of the 1940s and 1950s, until he over-reached himself with glass-fibre technology and with the production of a small sports car. This Berkeley Europa from 1953 had a bizarre steel-panelled body and was not a success.*

Left: *The low-cost Argosy Twelve, introduced by Panter in 1954. Constructed in a new works which was purely an assembly shop, its body was built of offcuts from the manufacture of the regular Berkeley ranges in the main factory.*

Right: *The Dinky Rambler was one of a 1950s breed of very lightweight caravans for towing either by small cars or by motorcycle and sidecar combinations. The 10 foot (3 metre) Rambler weighed 4³/4 cwt (241 kg) and featured a drop-down panel to allow a full-length bed.*

Above: *The last Car Cruiser to show any stylistic innovation was this stream-lined Lynx of 1953, with its panoramic windows and excellent view through. Low build and good headroom were achieved by running the floor below the chassis members. The floor itself was braced by wooden formers and was a stress-bearing part of the structure. The firm lasted into the 1960s, but by then the products had lost their character and much of their quality.*

Above: *The restyled Alperson Sprite of 1954 – an important step forward for the firm. Wrap-around front windows were a popular feature.*

Amphibious caravans have been a periodic obsession. This is the Otter from 1955. Powered by a $1^1/2$ horsepower British Anzani outboard motor, the plywood-panelled caravan was said to be capable of 4 knots when unbolted from its chassis and launched in the water.

Left: *The Paladin Corsair of 1955 was a pioneering user of glass-fibre, the entire upper half of the caravan being a GRP moulding. This allowed a more curvaceous shape.*

Right: *The Willerby Vogue was technically the most daring of the glass-fibre caravans, having a moulded GRP floor pan and no chassis as such – just two drawbar members fitting into grooves in the pan. But the promised weight of around 11 cwt (559 kg) for a 14 foot (4.3 metre) caravan proved hopelessly optimistic.*

ent suspension, which had been rare at the beginning of the decade: by 1962 around 50 per cent of manufacturers were using independent suspension of some kind.

In the meantime dampers increasingly became a standard fitting during the 1950s, and the quality of brakes and couplings increased significantly, while stabilisers – devices to damp out up-and-down and side-to-side movements of the caravan when on tow – also became more popular. The introduction in 1954 of the British Caravan Road Rally focused attention on the road behaviour of caravans and was a further influence on improved standards of chassis design.

Equipment improved, too. A new type of Calor gas cylinder simplified gas installations, refrigerators were incorporated, electrical systems were much improved, and awnings started to become a more accepted feature. Nevertheless, mains electricity installations in touring vans were still very rare and gas lighting was still the norm – with electric lighting via the car battery or an auxiliary battery still regarded as a back-up – and a hot water supply was most unusual in a caravan, as was an electric water-pump.

The most significant development of the 1950s was in the harnessing of new materials for the construction of caravans, most notably glass-fibre, more correctly known as glass-reinforced plastic (GRP), and caravan manufacturers were not far behind the motor industry in experimenting with it.

The chief advantage was that complex shapes, especially those incorporating curves, could be created in a way not economically possible with aluminium, and without the use of traditional coachbuilding skills. In addition, colour could be impregnated into the gel-coat, thereby eliminating painting. It was also thought that a glass-fibre caravan would be considerably lighter than an orthodox timber-framed alloy-panelled design, while at the same time being stronger, as well as rot-proof.

Paladin led the way in 1955, with a caravan the upper half of which was a glass-fibre moulding – an interesting and possibly sensible compromise. They were soon followed by Berkeley, with their Delight, and Willerby, with their Vista, both caravans being wholly GRP – including, on the Vista, the interior walls and the roof lockers.

Other manufacturers took up the new material, and in 1956 Willerby went one step further, with their Vogue. The most bizarrely streamlined of the GRP caravans, it incorporated a moulded glass-fibre floor, thereby eliminating the chassis, and even a moulded-in water tank on the drawbar.

But glass-fibre moulding was another new technique not easily mastered, and manufacturers who committed themselves fully to the new material soon discovered that problems encountered in the production processes exceeded the benefits. Furthermore, the claimed weight savings were illusory. Glass-fibre was a technical dead-end, and the only manufacturers to draw any benefit from it were those who used GRP purely for more shapely front and rear panels, and perhaps for the roof.

While all this was going on, sales of touring caravans were booming, and the number of caravanners was constantly increasing, with the Caravan Club's 1954 membership of 16,700 having doubled by the end of the decade. As Britain approached the consumer boom of the 1960s, there was a vibrancy in the caravan industry never before experienced.

Left: *By the end of the 1950s Bluebird caravans had considerably improved. This 1959-launched Touriste has an unusual downward slope to the side windows and a continental-style tubular drawbar. Independent suspension was used.*

Below: *The Cardiff firm of Fairholme became a medium-sized manufacturer in the mid-range sector but was taken over by Sam Alper's CI in 1965. This late 1950s model displays two-toning typical of the period and has Fairholme's characteristic 'wavy line' window trim.*

26

Eccles followed their rhomboid-shaped Sapphire/Moonstone range of 1961 with this new 'continental' shape for 1970, making extensive use of plastic mouldings, and with moulded ply roof members giving the shell much of its strength. Design work was by Ogle's Tom Karen.

INTO THE MODERN ERA: THE 1960s

The 1960s were years when the touring caravan flourished as never before. Following Britain's first International Caravan Show, at Earls Court in 1959, there were record annual sales of 46,000 touring and residential caravans in 1960, and from then on sales rocketed. As leisure time increased and formal touring caravan sites grew in number, the caravan evolved into a styled series-production consumer object for a new and affluent age.

The heady atmosphere of experimentation which had characterised the 1950s gave way to one of greater uniformity, but there were still some who bucked the trend, notably by bringing in designers from outside the industry.

The results were not necessarily what the public wanted. The Siddall Delta of 1961, designed at Conran by the future Ogle chief Tom Karen, was too unconventional inside and out to appeal, and much the same can be said of Karen's boldly styled Eccles Amethyst of 1969, successor to the equally distinctive Sapphire/Moonstone range of 1961. Unlike on the European mainland, where unusual and even bizarre designs seemed acceptable, in Britain, at least in the early years of the decade, it appeared that a design had to be conventional to succeed.

But if the style remained conservative, Britain's caravan manufacturers were at least making a variety of technological advances, as increased factory mechanisation spread through the industry.

Stretch-forming of aluminium panels and the use of pre-painted stove-enamelled aluminium sheet were important innovations and were accompanied by the growing use of thermoplastics for exterior and interior use, for items such as wheel-spats, window mouldings and washroom fittings. Photo-finished woods also made their appearance, as did various bright plastic interior fittings and finishes.

More crucially, expanded polystyrene came in as an insulating material and heralded the single most significant development in caravan technology since the introduction of aluminium panels – sandwich construction.

First seen in 1963 in the Sutherland Shannon Minor, sandwich construction replaced the traditional timber-framed alloy-clad form of construction with caravan walls made of a glued-together 'sandwich' of aluminium outer skin, polystyrene core and hardboard inner skin. The result was a light strong shell

27

Cheltenham built their first caravan, a motor van, in 1921 and remained in business until the early 1970s. Their later vans, up-market 'clubman' models, featured a front, rear and roof of glass-fibre. Looks were always traditional, as on this Fawn.

with only limited wood framing necessary.

Carlight tried a similar sandwich of GRP, polystyrene and melamine, but otherwise Sutherland's example was not followed, and it was not until the beginning of the 1980s that sandwich construction was adopted by the industry on a significant scale.

Meanwhile, the caravan was becoming a more comfortable place to spend one's holiday. Fluorescent lighting displaced the old gas mantles, a separate caravan battery became more popular, and by the end of the decade most caravans were designed to accept a small refrigerator. A new generation of flued gas-powered heaters was on the way, too, and electric water-pumps and electric control panels were not far in the future. Mains electrics, though, were largely confined to continental caravans until well into the 1980s.

Interior design became cleaner and more cohesive, too, with plainer fabrics, paler wood finishes, handle-less cupboards, and one-piece sink/drainer units; other details to come in during the decade were flush doorlocks, gas-cylinder boxes and under-floor insulation. In the process, even the cheapest and least well equipped caravans lost their austerity looks.

It was not just the caravans which changed in the1960s, however: the whole industry underwent a major transformation. The long-established makers simply failed to compete with the newcomers, and so Eccles was taken over in 1960 by Sam Alper's Sprite, Winchester closed down in 1959 (although another firm revived their designs), and Car Cruiser, its days as a high-class innovator long past, ceased production in 1965.

These disappearances were balanced by a

Mid 1960s Eccles Moonstone interior − an attempt at clean modern design. Note the contrasting wood finishes, the plain upholstery and carpet, and the simple clip-on single-leg table.

28

The American 'over-cab' style was tried by both Bluebird and Astral in the 1960s – without success. This is the 1964 model-year Bluebird Joie de Vivre six-berth, with double bed in the front overhang and a lift-up rear panel.

new generation of manufacturers that were to become well established – firms such as Mardon, Swift, Bailey, Abbey, Cavalier and Ace; and Hull became a new centre of the industry, with a number of businesses being set up in the area by former employees of Willerby and Astral.

But the largest production centre was the Suffolk town of Newmarket, home of Sam Alper's expanding business. Originally regarded as almost an upstart, Alper, creator of the Sprite, was by 1960 in a strong enough position to buy out Eccles, the oldest firm in the industry. After a brief spell of financial difficulty, in 1963 he took over the then industry leader, Bluebird. With combined annual sales of 22,000 caravans, the new enterprise, to become known as Caravans

International, or CI, accounted for over half the total UK production of caravans – not surprisingly, given that of the sixty or so manufacturers trading in 1963 only four or five turned out more than two thousand caravans a year.

By 1969 CI was the world's largest caravan manufacturer, following further takeovers in Britain and abroad and an impressive export programme – not to mention its absorption of various caravan equipment firms. It was also, at least in Britain, the sole force for innovation, as a result of Alper's passion for design and his belief in the importance of research and development work. As the 1970s began, however, other combines were forming to challenge CI's dominance.

By the 1960s the name 'Sprite' had become almost synonymous with 'caravan'. This is a Sprite Musketeer of the period, with the characteristic, and unique, 'swan's neck' roofline introduced in 1959 as a way of inexpensively giving form to the basic caravan shape.

The elevating-roof Sprite Compact of 1981 was costly to produce and not popular; claimed advantages were easier towing and the possibility of storing the caravan in an ordinary garage.

THE 1970s AND 1980s

The 1970s began with a boom, but by 1980 there was a definite slump, when sales fell away and only gradually rose thereafter. The weaker firms went out of business and, surprisingly, Sam Alper's CI went into receivership in 1982.

The key development of the 1970s was the rivalry for the popular caravan market, and Cosalt's Piper, ABI's Monza and Astral's Ranger competed vigorously for a share of the sector dominated by the Sprite. Astral ultimately withdrew, but Cosalt and ABI had established themselves as major producers by the end of the 1970s.

At the same time, as a result of canny niche-marketing, a new generation of respected firms arose from the 1960s boom, each with a clearly defined individual character. Swift made mid-range caravans with a quality touch; Avondale specialised in mid-to-upper-range caravans of high quality but affordable cost; Bessacarr, following its takeover of Astral's Cameo range, made top-of-range large caravans that promoted the twin-axle format, which was set to become one of the trends of the early 1980s.

The principal technical advance of this period was the introduction of sandwich construction at the beginning of the 1980s.

This allowed caravans to be lighter in weight and the strength of the new form of construction allowed chassis to become minimalist V-shaped frames as opposed to hefty steel-girder structures; even aluminium chassis were used despite the cost disadvantages. In addition, serious consideration was at last given to aerodynamics, and caravans were laboratory-tested for aerodynamic efficiency.

Caravans also became better equipped. Refrigerators and heaters increasingly became standard, hot water systems became more common, taking on modular form in the later 1980s, when the better furnished washrooms were fitted with slot-in 'cassette' lavatories, and mains electrics and electric control/distribution panels became *de rigueur* for middle to upper range caravans.

At the same time, though, a certain homogeneity became apparent. Technical advances led to the German manufacturer Al-Ko dominating the chassis and running-gear business, while there was a distinct lack of innovative design, doubtless because the two principal innovative caravans of the late 1970s, the Sprite Compact and the Bessacarr Admiral, had been commercial failures.

Left: *A late 1970s oddity: the Spacetrekker 520 claimed to offer the space of a 22 foot (6.7 metre) caravan within an overall length of 17 feet (5.2 metres). It featured two full-length beds in the elevating roof, twin doors, and a roll-out awning; equipment was lavish.*

Right: *Boldly styled inside and out by an independent design consultant, and a complete break with conventional practices, the Bessacarr Admiral was a total flop, with unsold vans in the maker's pound long after the model had been withdrawn.*

Left: *Abbey said they would put this unconventional-looking Lifestyle prototype of 1986 into production, but they never did so. Were the daring external styling and 'designer' interior likely to be unacceptable to the British public?*

FURTHER READING

The following books covering historic caravans are worth seeking out:

Whiteman, W. M., *The History of the Caravan,* Blandford Press, 1973.
Wilson, Nerissa, *Gypsies and Gentlemen,* Columbus, 1987.
Countless books on caravanning have been published over the years, however, and are worth looking for at autojumbles and in bookshops. In addition, *The Caravan Manual,* published in revised editions regularly since 1939 by *The Caravan* magazine, is a comprehensive guide to the caravanning scene at any given time; examples are quite easy to find. Other period titles worth looking out for include:

Bradman, W. A. G., *Caravan Construction,* Foyles, 1951.
Gordon-Stables, William, *The Cruise of the Land Yacht Wanderer,* 1886.
Cameron, L. C .R., *The Book of the Caravan.* Upcott Gill, 1907.
Hillyard, D. M., *The Caravan Family,* Blackie, 1938.
North, Arthur E., *The Book of the Trailer Caravan.* Pitman, first ed., 1952.
Smith, Bertram, *The Whole Art of Caravanning,* 1907.
Stone, J. Harris., *Caravanning and Camping Out,* first ed., 1913.
Ward, A. H. M., *Caravanning and Camping,* Pitman, first ed., 1931.

PLACES TO VISIT

There is no museum specifically devoted to caravans. However, certain museum collections, including those listed here, contain the occasional example. Intending visitors are advised to find out the opening times and that the relevant items are on display before making a special journey.

C. M. Booth Collection of Historic Vehicles, 63-7 High Street, Rolvenden, Cranbrook, Kent TN17 4LP. A 1930s Bampton expanding caravan.
    Telephone: 01580 241234. Website: www.morganmuseum.org.uk/C_M_Booth_Collection
City of Bristol Museum and Art Gallery, Queen's Road, Clifton, Bristol BS8 1RL.
    Gordon-Stables's The Wanderer. Telephone: 0117 922 3571.
Cotswolds Motor Museum, The Old Mill, Bourton-on-the-Water, Cheltenham, GL54 2BY.
    Telephone: 01451 821255. Website: www.cotswold-motor-museum.com
National Motor Museum, Beaulieu, Brockenhurst, Hampshire SO42 7ZN.
    Telephone: 01590 614650. Website: www.nationalmotormuseum.org.uk

CLUBS

There are very few clubs catering for historic caravans. The following are notable examples, which welcome enthusiasts of pre-1961 caravans:

Historic Caravan Club, contact: Roger Williams. 3 Heronfield Close, Redditch,
    Worcestershire B98 8QL. Email: enquire@hcclub.co.uk
    Website: www.historiccaravanclub.com
Period and Classic Caravan Club, contact: Jim Dick. 4 Crooked Well, Kington, Hereford
    HR5 3AF. Website: www.period-classic-caravan-club.co.uk